Ricky, Karim and Spit Nolan
ADVENTURE SHORT STORIES

Contents

Spit Nolan 3
by Bill Naughton
illustrated by Linda Clark

Thunderball Badshah 20
by Pratima Mitchell
illustrated by Nilesh Mistry

Ricky's Wheels 35
by Jenny Alexander
illustrated by Susan Hellard

Thunderball Badshah © Pratima Mitchell 2003
Ricky's Wheels © Jenny Alexander 2003
Series editors: Martin Coles and Christine Hall

PEARSON EDUCATION LIMITED
Edinburgh Gate
Harlow
Essex CM20 2JE
England

www.longman.co.uk

The right of Bill Naughton, Pratima Mitchell and Jenny Alexander to be identified as the authors of this work has been asserted by them in accordance with the Copyright, Designs and Patents Act, 1988.

We are grateful to Nelson Thornes Ltd for permission to reproduce the story 'Spit Nolan' by Bill Naughton from *The Goalkeeper's Revenge and Other Stories* by Bill Naughton.

All rights reserved. No part of this publication may be reproduced, stored in a retrieval system, or transmitted in any form or by any means, electronic, mechanical, photocopying, recording, or otherwise without either the prior written permission of the Publishers or a licence permitting restricted copying in the United Kingdom issued by the Copyright Licensing Agency Ltd, 90 Tottenham Court Road, London W1P 9HE.

First published 2003
ISBN 0582 79614 8

Illustrated by Linda Clark (The Black & White Line), Nilesh Mistry and Susan Hellard (Arena)

Printed in Great Britain by Scotprint, Haddington

The publishers' policy is to use paper manufactured from sustainable forests.

Spit Nolan
by Bill Naughton

Spit Nolan was a pal of mine. He was a thin lad with a face that was always pale, except for two rosy spots on his cheekbones. He had quick brown eyes, short, wiry hair, and we all knew that he had only one lung. He had had a disease which in those days couldn't be cured, unless you went away to Switzerland, which Spit certainly couldn't afford. He wasn't sorry for himself in any way, and he never had to go to school.

Spit was the champion trolley-rider. He had very good balance, and sharp wits, and he was very brave. No other boy could ever beat Spit on a trolley – and every lad had one.

Our trolleys were made for getting a good ride downhill at a fast speed. To make one you had to get a stout piece of wood about five feet in length and eighteen inches wide. Then you needed four wheels – large ones for the back and smaller ones for the front. We bought our wheels from the scrapyard. Now you had to get a poker and put it in the fire until it was red hot, and then burn a hole through the wood at the front. Usually it would take three or four attempts to get the hole bored through.

Through this hole you fitted the giant nut and bolt, for the steering. A piece of rope served for steering. Next you had to paint a name on it: *Invincible* or *Dreadnought*. That done, you then stuck your chest out, opened the back gate and wheeled your trolley out to face the world.

Spit spent most mornings trying out new speed gadgets on his trolley. Afterwards he would go off and have a spin down Cemetery Brew. This was a very steep road that led to the cemetery. Spit used to lie in wait for a coal cart, then he would hitch *Egdam* to the back to take it up the brew. *Egdam* was a name in memory of a girl called Madge, whom he had once met at Southport Sanatorium, where he had spent three happy weeks. Only I knew the meaning of it, for he had reversed the letters of her name to keep his love a secret.

It was the custom for lads to gather at the street corner on summer evenings and show off any new gadgets. Then, when Spit gave the sign, we used to set off for Cemetery Brew. There was scarcely any evening traffic on the roads in those days, so that we could have a good practice before our evening race. Spit, the champion, was always the last in the line of starters, though no matter how long a start he gave it seemed impossible to beat him. He knew

Brew: hill
Sanatorium: a kind of hospital

that road like the palm of his hand, every tiny lump or pothole, and he never came a cropper.

* * * * *

We were gathered at the street corner with our trolleys one evening when Ernie Haddock let out a hiccup of wonder: "Hey, chaps, wot's Leslie got?"

We all turned our eyes on Leslie Duckett, the plump son of the local publican. He approached us on a brand-new trolley. Such a magnificent trolley had never been seen! The riding board was of solid oak, four new wheels with tyres; a brake, a bell, a lamp, and a spotless steering-cord. In front was a plate on which was the name: *The British Queen*.

"It's called after the pub," remarked Leslie. Voices broke out:

"Where'd it come from?"

"How much was it?"

"Who made it?"

Leslie tried to look modest. "My dad had it specially made," he said, "by the gaffer of the Holt Works."

He was a nice lad, and now he wasn't sure whether to feel proud or ashamed. The fact was, nobody had ever had a trolley made by somebody else. Trolleys were swapped and so on, but no lad had ever owned one that had been made by other hands.

gaffer: boss

We went quiet now, for Spit had calmly turned his attention to it, and was examining *The British Queen* with his expert eye. First he tilted it, so that one of the rear wheels was off the ground, and after giving it a flick of the finger he listened intently.

"A beautiful ball bearing race," he remarked. "It runs like silk." Next he turned his attention to the body. "Grand piece of timber, Leslie – though a bit on the heavy side."

"I can pull it," said Leslie.

"You might find it a shade *front-heavy*," went on Spit, "which means it'll be hard on the steering unless you keep it well oiled."

"It's well made," said Leslie. "Eh, Spit?"

Spit nodded. "Aye," he said, "But –"

"But what?" asked Leslie.

"Do you want me to tell you?" asked Spit.

"Yes, I do," answered Leslie.

"Well, it's got none of *you* in it," said Spit.

"How do you mean?" says Leslie.

"Well, you haven't so much as given it a single tap with a hammer," said Spit. "That trolley will be a stranger to you to your dying day."

"How come," said Leslie, "since I *own* it?"
Spit shook his head. "You don't own it," he said, in a quiet, tone. "You own nothing in this world except those things you have taken a hand in the making of, or else you've earned the money to buy them."

Leslie sat down on *The British Queen* to think this one out. We all sat round, scratching our heads.

"You've forgotten to mention one thing," said Ernie Haddock to Spit, "what about the *speed?*"

"Going down a steep hill," said Spit, "she should hold the road well – an' with wheels like that she should certainly be able to shift some."

"Think she could beat *Egdam?*" asked Ernie.

"That," said Spit, "remains to be seen."

Ernie gave a shout. "A challenge race! *The British Queen* versus *Egdam*!"

"Not tonight," said Leslie. "I haven't got the proper feel of her yet."

"What about Sunday morning?" I said.

Spit nodded. "As good a time as any."

Leslie agreed. "By then," he said, "I'll be able to handle her."

* * * * *

Chattering like monkeys, eating bread, carrots, fruit, and bits of toffee, the entire gang of us made our way along the silent Sunday-morning streets for the

big race at Cemetery Brew. We were split into two sides.

Leslie, in his Sunday suit, walked ahead, with Ernie Haddock pulling *The British Queen*, and a bunch of supporters around.

Spit was in the middle of the group behind, and I was pulling *Egdam* and keeping the pace easy, for I wanted Spit to keep fresh. He walked in and out among us.

Chick Dale, a kid with a lisp, climbed up onto the spiked railings of the cemetery, and, reaching out with his thin fingers, snatched a yellow rose. He ran in front of Spit and thrust it into a small hole in his jersey.

"I pwesent you, with the wose of the winner!" he exclaimed.

"And I've a good mind to present you with a clout on the lug," replied Spit, "for pinching a flower from a cemetery. An' what's more, it's bad luck."

Seeing Chick's face, he said "On second

---

clout: a hard slap
lug: ear

thoughts, Chick, I'll wear it. Ee, wot a 'eavenly smell!"

Happily we went along, and Spit turned to a couple of lads at the back. "Hey, stop that whistling. Don't forget what day it is – folk want their sleep."

A faint sweated glow had come over Spit's face when we reached the top of the hill, but he was as calm as ever. Taking the bottle of cold water from his trolley seat, he put it to his lips and rinsed out his mouth in the manner of a boxer.

The two contestants were called together by Ernie. "No bumpin' or borin'," he said.

They nodded.

"The winner," he said, "is the first who puts the nose of his trolley past the cemetery gates."

They nodded.

"Now, who," he asked, "is to be judge?"

Leslie looked at me. "I've no objection to

Bill," he said. "I know he's straight."

I hadn't realised I was, I thought, 'but by heck I will be!'

"Ernie here," said Spit, "can be starter."

With that Leslie and Spit shook hands.

"Fly down to them gates," said Ernie to me. "I'll be setting 'em off dead on the stroke of ten o'clock."

I hurried down to the gates. I looked back and saw the supporters lining themselves on either side of the road. Leslie was sitting upright on *The British Queen*. Spit was settling himself to ride belly down. Ernie Haddock, handkerchief raised in the right hand, eyes gazing down on a watch in the left, was counting them off.

"Five – four – three – two – one – off!"

Spit was away like a shot. That toe push sent him clean ahead of Leslie. There were shouts from his supporters, and groans from Leslie's. I saw Spit move straight to the middle of the road camber. Then I ran ahead to take up my position at the winning post.

When I turned again I was surprised to see that Spit had not increased the lead. In fact, it seemed that Leslie had begun to gain on him. He had settled himself into a crouched position, and those perfect wheels combined with his extra weight were bringing him up with Spit. Not that it seemed possible he could ever catch him. For Spit, lying flat on his trolley, gliding over the rough patches, looked to me as though he were a bird that might suddenly fly clean into the air.

The runners along the side could no longer keep up with the trolleys. And now, as they came to the very steepest part, there was no doubt that Leslie was gaining. Spit had never ridden better. Yet Leslie, riding the rougher part of the road, was actually drawing level.

Dead level they sped into the final stretch.

camber: a slight upward curve towards the centre of a road

Spit's slight figure was poised fearlessly on his trolley. Thundering beside him, anxious but determined, came Leslie.

He was actually drawing ahead. I kept my eyes fastened clean across the road as they came belting past the winning post.

First past was the *The British Queen*. I saw that first. Then I saw the heavy rear wheel jog over a hole and strike Spit's front wheel – sending him in a swerve across the road. Suddenly then, from nowhere, a charabanc came speeding round the wide bend.

Spit was straight in its path. Nothing could avoid the crash. I gave a cry of fear as I saw the

charabanc: a large bus

heavy solid tyre of the front wheel hit the trolley. Spit was flung up and his back hit the radiator. Then the driver stopped dead.

I got there first. Spit was lying on the road on his side. His face was white and dusty, and coming out between his lips, and trickling down his chin, was fresh red blood. Scattered all about him were yellow rose petals.

"Not my fault," I heard the driver shouting. "I didn't have a chance. He came straight at me."

The next thing we were surrounded by women who had got out of the charabanc. And then Leslie and all the lads came up.

"Somebody send for an ambulance!" called a woman.

"I'll run an' tell the gatekeeper to telephone," said Ernie Haddock.

"I hadn't a chance," the driver explained to the women.

"Don't move him," said the driver to a woman who had bent over Spit. "Wait for the ambulance."

"Hush up," she said. She knelt and put a silk scarf under Spit's head. Then she wiped his mouth with her little handkerchief.

He opened his eyes. Glazed they were, as though he couldn't see. A short cough came out of him, then he looked at me and his lips moved.

"Who won?"

"Thee!" blurted out Leslie. "Tha just licked me. Eh, Bill?"

"Aye," I said, "old Egdam just pipped *The British Queen*."

Spit's eyes closed again. The women looked at each other. They nearly all had tears in their eyes. Then Spit looked up again, and his wise, knowing look came over his face. After a minute he spoke in a whisper:

"Liars. I can remember seeing Leslie's back wheel hit my front 'un. I didn't win – I lost." He stared upward for a few seconds, then his eyes twitched and shut.

The driver kept repeating how it wasn't his fault, and next thing the ambulance came. Nearly all the women were crying now, but I couldn't believe he was dead. I had to go into the ambulance with the attendant. I went up the step and sat down inside and looked out the little window as the driver slammed the doors. Chick Dale was lifting the smashed-up *Egdam* onto *The British Queen*. People with bunches of flowers in their hands stared after us as we drove off. Then I heard the ambulance man asking me

Spit's name. Then he touched me on the elbow with his pencil and said, "Where did he live?"

I knew then. That word 'did' struck right into me. But for a minute I couldn't answer. I had to think hard, for the way he said it made it suddenly seem as though Spit Nolan had been dead and gone for ages.

Thunderball Badshah
by Pratima Mitchell

Karim could feel his skin burning with excitement. It wasn't the kind of thrill he got when he went to the circus or a fair. It wasn't the thrill he got when he scored a goal. This excitement came from having just two hours to finish making his kite, *Thunderball Badshah* – Thunderball the Emperor. He had to try a test flight and get ready for the big day tomorrow.

The big kite-flying competition started in Jaipur the next day. Karim dreamed of winning the junior section. If he won, his Uncle Hamid had promised to take him on a trip to Delhi to the airport, where he could watch planes take off and land for a whole afternoon. Karim's father said he would match the prize money so he could have a new bike.

Besides, he had to beat that toad Keshav next door. Keshav was always boasting about his brother who was a student in America.

Karim looked at his watch. Once the sun went down he'd have to pack up and go home to his family's tiny apartment with babies and beds and cooking and brothers and sisters running in and out, and Amma shouting and sending him out to the grocer downstairs. There'd be nowhere to work on *Thunderball*.

So he had to make good use of this time in Mira's courtyard, which was right under the ancient city wall.

On the ground was the kite frame – sticks of finest bamboo tied together with white cotton. He was just putting the kite together when something flew past his ear. He dropped the scissors and swore in his head. Mira was throwing potato peelings at him. Sitting high above on the old wall, she teased, "Let me, let me …"

The wall had been built hundreds of years ago to guard the city against invaders. It ran all along one side of Mira's house. From the top Mira had a fantastic view of the old city, with its higgledy-piggledy back lanes full of noise and excitement.

"Let me, let me …" she sang. Karim had to grit his teeth to stop himself shouting at her.

"Let you what?" he snapped.

"Let me have a go at killing kites tomorrow," Mira begged.

He turned his head to look up.

"If you keep on worrying me, there will be no competition for us. Look how much work there is to finish … just leave me alone for now. Okay?"

He had to be careful not to annoy her, or else there'd be nowhere for him to work. Mira had her uses. She could see into Keshav's courtyard, and she told Karim what Keshav was doing. Today Keshav was fixing tiny balls of soft lead to his kite frame. Launching it would be hard, but the lead balls would give it terrific balance and steering.

But Karim had a trick or two up his sleeve. He had made a deal with the sweet-maker round the corner of the lane. The sweet-maker had let Karim steam the bamboo sticks over his huge pot of boiling water to make them more bendy.

Now Karim bent the crossbar into a curve. Tomorrow *Thunderball* was going to swoop on the back of air currents! Lord of the skies, it would first hover like a bird of prey, and then … zap! *Thunderball* would cut the other kites. Last year Keshav had cut down three kites. Karim knew he could beat that score. He could almost hear the roar of the crowd all over Jaipur, "Karim is the champion! Karim is the champion!"

He came back to earth when another potato peeling hit his ear.

"Say you'll let me fly *Thunderball* tomorrow, say it!"

It was too much. Just because she let him work in her courtyard didn't give Mira the right to bully him. Anyway, girls never flew kites in the competition. They just never had done. What on earth would his friends say?

Mira's mother called from inside the kitchen, "Lazy girl! Are those potatoes peeled?"

Mira took a last look down. She heard honking horns, tinkling rickshaw bells, fruit-sellers, a wedding band practising wonky wrong notes. Bright green parrots flashed past her and the smell of frying bhajis tickled her nose. She tried to make out if her grandfather's camel cart was coming. She could see a few pompous-looking camels, even an elephant or two, but no sign yet of Grandfather.

But every year Grandfather came for the kite-flying festival, because he'd been a champion in his youth. He came with his cart full of sacks of presents from his village: yellow lentils, good wheat flour, cornmeal, golden raw sugar, sugar cane sticks for Mira, and a basket of potatoes and onions. Tomorrow, he and Mira would climb up to their rooftop and together watch the red, green, purple and yellow kites dancing like butterflies in the clear blue sky.

* * * * *

Karim held up his finished kite to catch the last rays of the sun. He was ready for the test flight.

He dodged Mira, and climbed up the steps to the top of the wall.

Falcons glided above. He'd watched the birds for hours to try and work out how they mastered air currents. He wanted *Thunderball* to fly like a falcon.

Karim waited for the first friendly breeze, then launched his kite. Up and up it soared. He let it ride for a while, and then started to reel it in again – like playing with a fish in the river. No hurry, nice and easy, gently, gently.

But, all of a sudden, a freak wind, with a sting of desert sand in its tail, caught the kite and brought it down towards the middle of the courtyard. It fell like a shot bird, getting stuck in the very top branches of the guava tree. Karim's heart also fell. He couldn't tell whether the kite was damaged. He couldn't reach it because it was so high up in the branches. Even if they'd had a ladder tall enough he couldn't have climbed it. His left leg didn't have enough strength because he'd had polio when he was small.

Just then, the gentle clunk-clunk of camel bells sounded in the lane outside the courtyard. "Dadaji!" Mira shouted. She ran to tell her grandfather the bad news.

Dadaji climbed down from his cart. "I saw, I saw. It was flying well. But where will you find a ladder at this time of night?"

Mira's mother brought a bucket of water and Dadaji sloshed it on the camel's big dusty feet. He tied it up under the guava tree. The camel smiled when it saw the guava leaves.

Mira put her hands on her hips. "Karim, I can get your kite down, but I'll only do it on one condition."

"Which is?"

"That I share the kite-flying with you tomorrow, and you take me with you to watch the planes at the airport in Delhi."

"What? Are you out of your mind?" Karim's mouth stayed open. He could not believe her boldness. Anyway, she was just a bigmouth. How on earth would she get up the tree?

"Hup hup heee!" Mira thumped the camel and it folded its front legs and sat down. She climbed on its back. "Hup hup hooo!" and the camel stood up again with Mira on top.

"If I stand up, I can get the kite. Come on, Karim, promise, or I'm coming down again."

"It's blackmail!" he shouted angrily.

"Go on, Karim, don't be silly or you'll lose your kite. Say yes to Mira," said Mira's mum.

"You'll allow her to go to Delhi with me?"

"Yes, why not? You're friends, aren't you?"

"Oh, all right then. But I'll have the first turn! You can have a go after I've brought down four kites."

"We have two witnesses," Mira said. "Don't you dare change your mind!"

She stood up slowly, wobbling a little on her bare feet. It was a brave thing to do. Gently she untangled *Thunderball* and sat down on the saddle looking at the kite. "It's fine," she said, handing it back to Karim. She jumped off the camel and gave it a piece of raw sugar.

* * * * *

The competition was on the last day of winter. In Jaipur, everyone loves the winter months because the sun is so comforting, and the flowers bloom. The competitors were all gathered on their rooftops adjusting their kites. The judges waited for the last stroke of nine from the clock and a gunshot went off to start of the competition.

Karim let Mira hold *Thunderball* to launch it. Away it went, spinning higher and higher, with Karim dodging about on the roof steering it. He set his first target and stalked it. With a tug of his string he guided *Thunderball* to cut into a white kite. Down it came.

Dadaji and Mira whooped happily. They
could see Keshav on his own
rooftop with his family,
including his brother from
America.

Karim followed his first
hit by bringing down two
others – a yellow, and a blue. He
launched *Thunderball* again.
Mira held the spool for him; she
followed his every move. This
time Keshav turned his attention
to Karim's kite. Keshav was a
very skilful kite-flyer.

Thunderball and Keshav's
orange kite were flying at the
same height,
not too close, waiting
for the right moment
to strike.

Quietly, Mira's voice sounded right behind Karim. "Kill it," she said. "Go on, *now!*" Her timing was perfect, because when Karim tugged his string to swiftly change direction, he caught Keshav by surprise. In a split second, the orange kite came down. There were groans and shouts of disappointment from Keshav's family.

"That's four – now it's my turn," Mira said.

But Karim was nervous. Keshav and he had drawn – four kites each. "I have to get more than *him*," he said.

"A promise is a promise," Mira shouted.

She snatched the string from him and handed him the spool.

"Only three minutes more," the judge said.

Mira launched *Thunderball* into the air.

The breeze was stronger now and it climbed up true and straight. Mira handled the kite with an expert flick of her wrist making it dart here and there.

Karim had to admit that Mira's skills weren't bad. She took risks like him, and in no time she'd brought down one more.

"End of time!" the judge said, writing down the score.

Karim's *Thunderball* won the junior section with five hits. Keshav was second with four hits.

Karim bought his bike, a red one with ten gears and a fancy horn that drove everyone mad.

Uncle Hamid took Mira and Karim to the airport, where they watched dozens and dozens of planes taking off and landing.

"I'll be on one of those when I'm older," Karim said to Mira.

"I'll be *flying* them when I'm older," she said.

"Now why didn't I think of that?" Karim said to himself.

Being good at flying kites didn't mean that she was going to be good at flying aeroplanes. He'd have to keep his eye on her to make sure she didn't get too big for her sandals!

Ricky's Wheels
by Jenny Alexander

Every day after school we race home through the park, Ricky and me, and nine times out of ten Ricky wins. When we first started doing it, it used to be ten times out of ten, but then I stopped taking pity on him on the uphill slope, because he certainly didn't take pity on me on the long roll downhill towards the lake.

Sometimes people give me a dirty look when they see Ricky pushing up the hill. "Shame on you!" they say. "Why aren't you helping your friend?" That makes me and Ricky really cross. If they took the trouble to watch him before they started spouting off, maybe they wouldn't be so quick to wag their fingers at me over his head.

That chair is like part of his body, and wheeling

is as easy for him as walking is for me. He doesn't get tired on the flat, any more than I do, and when he's going uphill he paces himself. On a roll, he's like a long-distance swimmer, with all the power in his arms and upper body as he glides along.

When he had his old chair he used to let me have a go on it sometimes, but I was rubbish! He doesn't let me go on his new one. It's blue and silver, and it's made of aluminium, so it's light and easy to steer.

Last Thursday was one of those days when a well-meaning person spoilt the race. Ricky and I had just finished playing football with some other boys in our class. I was a bit tired, but as Ricky does the reffing he was as fresh as a daisy. I could see the bandstand ahead and Ricky not far enough behind for comfort. Suddenly this old woman stepped out in front of me, blocking the path. "You should be ashamed of yourself, young man!" she said. "What about your friend?"

My friend looked okay to me, pushing on up towards us, grinning.

I didn't want to be rude, but I didn't want to hang around either, so I ducked past the woman and raced on. Too late! I was only halfway down to the lake when Ricky went gliding past.

When I got to the Carlton Street gate he was waiting for me. "Hard cheese, Sam!" he said, grinning. "Shall we go back to yours now and play Road Race, or are you too scared I'll beat you?"

He was joking, of course. Nobody beats me at Road Race

We went round to the back of the house because we've got a ramp that my dad built when Ricky first had his accident. It was ages ago, but I can still remember it as if it was yesterday. I can remember when Ricky used to walk on his feet, which is a very strange thought. We were halfway up this cliff on a beach somewhere. Our two families were on a day out together. We'd done the hard bit, and then Ricky goes, "Race you to the top!" Some things never change.

The house was empty, but the computer was on. Abbie wasn't there. She must've come home and gone out again. Typical Abbie! She's supposed to be in charge until Mum and Dad get in, so it's just as well I don't really need looking after. Some people hate their big sisters, but I think Abbie's okay. I don't mind that she thinks she's cool and she talks down to me quite a lot; I think it's funny. She's in Year 9, but I know she still sleeps with her teddy!

Ricky was ready to play Road Race. You

would have thought he'd be really good at it. I mean, it's what he does all the time, slowing and steering round corners, speeding up on the straight. But he just makes stupid mistakes.

He had got bogged down in the mud when we heard a blip, and noticed that Abbie was on Net Messenger. I never normally see who she is chatting to on-line. "Let's have a look," I said.

Ricky didn't think we should, but then he hasn't got a big sister. I paused the game and clicked on the icon.

```
teenhero:  wanna meet me, then?
abz:       where?
teenhero:  the cafe at the canal
           centre
abz:       ok. bus leaves in 5. cu soon
vikz:      hi
vikz:      hello
vikz:      is anyone there?
```

"That's where she is, then," Ricky said. "Who's Teenhero?"

I shrugged. "Let's go to her list of contacts and see if we can work it out."

Abbie's friends had all just shortened their own names and put a z on the end. There was Emz, Vikz, Sooz, Carlz, and Gemz. And then there was Anto. I frowned. I thought she had got rid of him ages ago. She had met him in a chatroom and they had talked about music for a while. He said he was fifteen, blonde and keen on the same bands as her, but I always thought there was something fishy about him. Now here he was among Abbie's contacts. And then there was Teenhero. Had Abbie picked him up in a chatroom, too? If she had, surely she wouldn't be stupid enough to go and meet him?

Ricky scrolled back through the conversation …

"It can't be one of her friends," Ricky said. "They all know where she lives." I was starting to have a really bad feeling. I got out my mobile and sent Abbie a text. She would probably just tell me to get lost, but I didn't care. A few seconds later, we heard Abbie's mobile bleep in her room upstairs. For some reason, the sound of Abbie's mobile in her empty bedroom really freaked me out.

"Let's think this through," Ricky said. "Let's stay calm and think it through."

But I didn't feel calm, and when I thought about it all I could see were newspaper headlines in my head, bad scary headlines that I couldn't blot out.

The clock said 4.35. There wasn't another bus for twenty minutes. It would be quicker to go on foot, especially if I took the shortcut.

"What are you thinking?" Ricky asked.

"I'm going down there to make sure she's okay," I said, jumping up. "It'll only take fifteen minutes if I run."

"It's downhill nearly all the way," goes Ricky. "If it takes you fifteen minutes, I bet I can do it in ten."

He didn't wait for me to answer, but started backing away from the computer and turning his chair. "Go on then," he said. "I'll catch up with you."

I ran out the front door and sprinted up to the corner. Then I turned into Carlton Road and raced along the edge of the park. When I got to the Mini-Mart I glanced back, but there was no sign of Ricky yet.

I set off again down Hanger Lane. What if Teenhero turned out to be some weirdo? What if there weren't many people around at the canal centre, and Abbie had no one to turn to for help?

By the time I got to the Cut I was really tired. The Cut is a wide straight path that runs between two big houses. There is a concrete post in the middle to stop cars going down it. I leaned on the post for a few moments, trying to catch my breath. If Ricky took the corner too fast he could be in trouble. But Ricky would have to look after himself.

I ran through the Cut to the end, and turned into the alley, glancing back just in time to see Ricky slide his chair neatly between the wall and the post. The alley is much narrower than the cut.

After a couple of hundred metres, I heard Ricky's wheels and

jumped clear just in time. He shot past me, going too fast, but I knew the path flattened out later so he would have chance to slow down before he got to the towpath at the bottom.

The canal path was straight and flat. I could just make out the canal shopping centre, beyond the bridge.

My feet felt like lumps of lead, but seeing the canal centre spurred me on.

Soon I could see the café with its picnic tables outside. There were loads of people about, but I couldn't see Abbie among them.

I overtook Ricky just before the bridge. There were some steps up to the bridge, and I knew he would need a hand, but I didn't want to stop.

"You go on," he yelled. "Don't wait!"

I raced up the steps and over the bridge. I burst into the café. Everyone looked round. The place was full of people. But Abbie wasn't there.

Suddenly, I heard a loud whistle. I went back outside and onto the bridge. I saw Ricky on the far side, with his referee's whistle in his mouth. He let it drop out and yelled at me.

"I know where they are!" he said. "I saw them go into the gardens!"

I ran through the arch into the gardens. Abbie was sitting on a bench with a boy. He was about the same age as her. I had half expected him to be at least fifty, with a beer gut and a seedy smile. I yelled her name, and they both looked round. I thought I recognised him from somewhere.

Abbie was furious. "What are you doing here?" she said.

I was still working out what to say, when Ricky arrived.

"Are you two spying on me?" Abbie demanded.

She sat back and crossed her arms. She didn't have to say a word. We told her everything – about reading her messages, and trying to guess who Teenhero was, and thinking she'd gone to meet some creep off the Internet. She was really angry. "What kind of an idiot do you take me for?" she said. "If you must know, this is my boyfriend, Jason. He's in my class."

"Your boyfriend?" I said. "Why didn't you tell me you had a new boyfriend?"

"Because I knew you'd just be embarrassing like you were last time. Now go home and grow up!"

As we left the gardens I looked back and I saw Abbie and Jason holding hands, not talking to each other, which is exactly what she's like with all her boyfriends. I felt a bit of a fool.

* * * * *

Thinking about it, I could understand why Abbie was cross

with me, but I couldn't see why Ricky seemed cross, too. He hardly said a word to me all the way home.

The game was still on the computer. Ricky finished his race. He flew round the course in record time, not making a single mistake. I couldn't believe it – he beat me!

"Are you angry with me?" I asked.

He nodded. "It was downhill nearly all the way to the canal centre, but you got there first," he said. "You've been letting me win when we race through the park. You must've been."

I shook my head. Had I been letting him win? I didn't mean to. "Well, what about Road Race?" I said. "It looks like you've been letting me win at that!"

We looked at each other in surprise. Maybe we had been slowing down for each other.

And maybe that was okay.